How Can I Fix the Problem?

Solving Problems

Emiliya King

SOCIAL AND EMOTIONAL LEARNING FOR THE REAL WORLD™

Rosen Classroom™

You have a problem.
How can you fix it?

Solving problems is
an important skill.
You can do it step by step!

Imagine your class needs
a new fish tank.
The old tank is broken.

First, find out what the problem is. You need money for the fish tank.

You know the problem.
Now, you can make a plan!
What's the next step?

Look at your choices.
What can you do?
What will happen?

Your class can raise money.
You can have a bake sale.
You can sell cupcakes.

Make a plan.
Who will bake the cupcakes?
Who will sell them?

Your plan worked!
You made enough money
for a new fish tank.

Solving problems can be easy.
You just have to take it
step by step!

Words to Know

cupcake

fish tank